CW01085206

THE COCKTAIL BAR

Notes for an Owner & Operator

Chall Gray

White Mule Press a division of the
American Distilling Institute
PO Box 577
Hayward, CA 94541
whitemulepress.com

Copyright 2018 © Chall Gray

All rights reserved.

ISBN 978-0-9968277-9-9

To Lucia. I couldn't imagine doing anything without you.

CONTENTS

I n my mid-twenties, after spending several years produc-
ing theatre and music, I had grandiose plans to open a
black box performance venue, with a small restaurant
and bar attached. I had an idea in my head that the patrons,
crew and cast would hang out before and after the show, and
it would be a gathering place for those of us who worked in
theatre, music and art. I knew next to nothing about what I
was doing (at the time I'd never worked in a restaurant, or
even set foot behind a bar), but was supremely motivated to
make things happen.

I planned, figured out financing, and worked furiously
for years. We had lots of exciting shows, served a ton of
great drinks at the bar, and sent many delicious meals out of
the kitchen, but ultimately it didn't work.

The way I'd set up the model was deeply flawed. And,
worse than that, I had badly misjudged the location. The
rent was far higher than the model I'd set up could support.
What I thought was a hot neighborhood about to take off is
now, a decade later, an area that still hasn't taken off.

In the months after we closed the bar, I swore off the
restaurant and bar business, started looking for jobs and
tried to figure out what to do next. A job offer with a small
chain of local bars came along and I took it, thinking it
would pay for the mortgage while I figured out the next
step. Then a funny thing happened. It wasn't long before

I realized how much I loved the bar industry, specifically cocktails and spirits. I ended up opening several bars for that company before leaving to pursue my own projects.

Along the way a friend and colleague asked me to recommend a book on opening bars that he could study. The best thing on my own shelves was Harry Johnson's Bartender's Manual, a superb book, but with an original publication date of 1882 there are a few areas that aren't in step with today's market. Most of the books that showed up on Amazon searches were geared toward running high-volume nightclubs, which didn't fit the bill either. That started me toward creating the book that you're now holding.

In preparing this manuscript, I've spoken to some of the top bar owners from across America. My interview subjects ranged from small-market owners with less than 1,000 square feet of total space, to the leaders of large bar/restaurant groups with multiple units and hundreds of employees. My goal was to get as many perspectives as possible on what it takes to be a successful bar operator. After these many interviews I've done my best to combine the wisdom, advice, mistakes and experiences of the industry into one volume.

Ultimately, this book is meant to be an overview of what goes into designing, opening and running a cocktail bar or program. This is definitely not designed to be your sole resource for opening a bar. Frankly, any individual section would be longer than this entire book if one were trying to cover it thoroughly enough to prepare you for what it takes to open and operate your own place.

You may be interested in opening a bar right now, and then find by the end of the book that you've changed your mind. Or perhaps it's the opposite, and your notes and plans will grow as you go through the sections. Either way, I hope you find something useful in here, and I hope you enjoy a cocktail or two while you read.

Cheers,
Chall Gray
Asheville, NC
November, 2017

Four out of five. Four out of five new food and beverage businesses fail within five years of opening. You may have heard this oft-quoted statistic before, but it's worth stopping and thinking about for a moment. 80% of the ventures by people crazy enough to try this industry fail. That's an incredible amount of lost money, time, energy, and who knows what else. So what do they all get wrong? Why do so many fail?

As someone that has opened a number of bars that have done well (and a couple that didn't do so well), I would posit that most of the reasons that bars and restaurants fail can be summed up in five words. *Lack of knowledge and preparation.*

Chances are good that if you're reading this you have some interest in someday opening your own bar, or perhaps you're already starting to plan it. This industry isn't one that's especially easy or simple for a newcomer to learn, and cocktail bars require an even higher level of specialized knowledge. The sad fact is this: the fate of many bars and restaurants are decided long before the doors open—by fundamental decisions about concept, location and business model.

Opening a bar is a difficult, often grueling task. Owners spend months or years working long hours planning, preparing and opening the bar, only to find that the relief of opening can be short lived, and the demands of an owner are sometimes even greater thereafter. The hours even longer. The stresses even more continual. Martin Cate, owner of Smugglers Cove, Whitechapel and other world-famous bars, said that being able to fix plumbing issues (usually late on a weekend night), was absolutely key to success as an owner in the bar industry.

Sometimes there are long stretches where you might spend more time dealing with broken refrigeration equipment, plumbing leaks or other malfunctions than you do even seeing the inside of the bar, much less drinking at it.

In fact, it should be said right here: if one of your reasons for wanting to open a bar is to spend evenings drinking at your bar, surrounded by friends, then just find a bar you like and go there with your friends every evening. Chances are good your bank account will look much better in the end.

Even if you're opening your bar based on clear reasoning and intentions, it's still a world of rising costs and rising rents. Profit margins in the food and beverage industry are lower than those of many other businesses with similar gross sales. Those trends show no signs of reversing. In addition, cocktail programs often require many expenditures, both in terms of capital and ongoing costs, that a neighborhood pint house or wine bar doesn't. Jeff Bell, who runs PDT (Please Don't Tell) in New York City, one of the leading bars in the world, said it succinctly: "You shouldn't get into this business to get rich."

So, to recap, the odds are that you will fail, and if you don't fail, well, the odds are good that you still won't make much money. Oh, and you're probably going to work yourself absolutely to the bone. In truth, several of the bar owners I interviewed for this book questioned their own sanity in pursuing this as a career.

At this point, if nothing else, we've clearly established that this isn't the easiest profession out there. If you were looking for an easy business to start, you've got the wrong book.

But, let's say you weren't just looking for something easy. When I think back upon the jobs that I've had that felt easy, they stand out as the ones that were the least challenging, and the least exciting. They also felt stale and boring relatively quickly.

Bar ownership demands a diverse skill set, and for those that happen to have (or develop) that skill set, it is constantly exciting, challenging, and fun as well as immensely rewarding. Bar ownership demands that you solve an ever-changing array of unique problems. It also gives you the amazing satisfaction of seeing happy patrons enjoying an experience, and knowing that they will return based on that experience. A cohesive bar team is a joy to watch, and even more so to be a part of, and lead. It also happens to be a career in which tasting different variations on an Old Fashioned or Manhattan is part of your workday, which never hurt anyone's job satisfaction.

Basically, for many of us that do it, being a bar operator is one of the greatest professions in the world, and we find it hard to imagine ourselves doing anything else.

Within the larger bar ecosystem, cocktail bars are a much smaller subset. The profit margins aren't intrinsically higher than those in a shot-and-beer place or neighborhood dive bar (often less, actually). It's a significantly more labor intensive endeavour than a wine or beer bar, and very few

What is the one trait that is most important to being a successful owner?

"The best operators are great at solving unique problems."
—Danny Shapiro, Scofflaw, Chicago

"Patience, fearlessness, and subversion of your own ego."

"Being able to stay calm as unexpected things go wrong every day."

"What you're really doing as an owner is that you're creating a culture, and you have to embody that for the staff and lead by example. You have to hold yourself to a higher standard."

"Consistency and attention to detail."

"Adaptability."

"Persistence."

other types of establishment require such a broad amount of requisite knowledge on the part of staff.

But if you're reading this, there's a good chance you already understand the spell a great cocktail can cast, and why more and more people are taking up the mantle of serving carefully considered and well-made mixed drinks.

A decade ago it was hard to find a well-made cocktail in some larger cities, much less in smaller regional markets.

Those times have changed. Now you can go to pretty much any city of a decent size, all across thve country, and find at least one or two bartenders who know not to put soda and fluorescent cherries in an Old Fashioned, or won't make the mistake of shaking your Manhattan. And it only continues to get better. With the rise of craft beer and spirits more consumers than ever before understand and appreciate the quality of small-batch, artisan products, drinks and establishments.

"The craft cocktail movement was based on people doing things in a great way."
—Neal Bodenheimer, Cure, New Orleans

Much more talented writers than yours truly have chronicled the resurgence of the cocktail that has occurred in the most recent decades, and if you're interested in learning more about it (it's quite a fascinating story), I recommend Robert Simonson's *A Proper Drink*.

And because of the talented bar men and women chronicled in Simonson's book, and many others, you can now find bars that serve a well-made cocktail from Savannah to Santa Monica, and everywhere in between. You can find these cocktails in restaurants, hotels, bars, distilleries, coffee shops and many more types and styles of establishments. And, hopefully, in a bar of your own someday as well.

PLANNING

[PART ONE]

YOUR BAR AS A CONCEPT

Within the cocktail bar world there are many, many different styles and types of bars—from tiki bars to gin emporiums, proto-dive bars, whiskey bars, pre-prohibition speakeasies, mezcalerias, bitters palaces, and on and on. There are bars built around a wealth of themes—everything from architects to specific places and eras in history. There are also many bars that just work to serve great cocktails to the neighborhood around them, without being fussy or gimmicky about it.

As cocktails have exploded in popularity over the last two decades, you can now find a good drink in many places beyond just a traditional bar. Great cocktails can be enjoyed in restaurants, airports, distillery tasting rooms (in states that allow it), hotels, and many other concepts. You may be planning to open what will surely be a new beacon of cocktail wizardry in a metropolis that already has several notable tippling houses, or perhaps you're planning to be the first bar to serve good cocktails in a smaller, regional market. (For the sake of simplicity we will use the example of a bar throughout the book, even though you may be planning to integrate cocktails into a restaurant, venue or other type of operation.) Either way, you must be absolutely clear on what the intention behind your bar is.

By intention, what I mean is the concept, theme and focus of the bar. Depending on your situation you may or may not implement what we discuss in this chapter prior to finding a location. But in our hypothetical timeline we will assume that you will search for and find a location after settling on the concept for the bar.

Concept & Focus

So, what do you want your bar to be? Do you want to have the biggest whiskey selection around, leather chairs and attentive, upscale service? Be known for excellently made classics? Establish a tiki haven with a fun party atmosphere, hundreds of miles from the nearest large body of water? Introduce a cocktail program to an already existing restaurant to bring in new customers? Open a great neighborhood bar that offers a well-rounded menu of great drinks, but focuses on service? Add cocktails to your distillery tasting room? Regardless of where your ambitions fall, it is key to answer the following questions.

What's the Main Concept?

Do you want to focus on a menu of straightforward classics, served in a casual atmosphere? Create an immersive Tiki experience?

You may want to focus on a particular spirit, like mezcal or gin, or on creating an atmosphere evocative of a specific place (like an Irish pub) or era (such as a speakeasy with prohibition-era style). Perhaps it's filling a niche within a neighborhood, or focusing on a certain style of service.

None of these things are mutually exclusive, but it is very important to have absolute clarity on the main concept and focus of the business. There will be numerous decisions later in the opening process, from table layouts to staffing levels, that will be dictated by your answer here.

The process to get there is often time consuming, but very worthy of your time. I've often filled dozens of notebook pages working out the details of a concept.

The main concept, once complete, can usually be distilled into one sentence. Once finished, that sentence should clearly delineate the core areas of focus for the business, and can be referred to during important decisions later in the life of the business.

Do your best to think through every aspect of how you imagine a busy night at the bar.

What Is Necessary For the Concept?
This is an extension of the first question, but will likely (and should) be the longest answer you'll provide to any question in this book. You're trying to lay out as many details of the concept as possible. Be as thorough as possible.

How big should the space be? What type of music will typically be playing? Will it be turned up loud or usually low and set a mood? How big will the cocktail list be?

Will the bartenders be wearing a t-shirt from their favorite punk band, a logo'd shirt from the bar or a dress shirt? How extensive will the food selection be? Cloth napkins or paper? Table service? Door guy checking id's, hostess seating patrons or do they just walk in and order at the bar? The more detail you have here the better.

Do your best to think through every aspect of how you imagine a busy night at the bar. How will it work? What do you want the customers to experience? What is necessary to make that happen?

Can You Describe Your Target Customer Demographic(s), and What's Important to Them?

Are you going to cater to a young, hip crowd? Better have one or two cheap beer choices that have indie cred. Do you expect it to be an older, more affluent crowd? The cheap beer is less important, but now it's more important to have a wine list that features some interesting varietals.

The list goes on, but the point is to identify what you think will be your key customer bases, and make sure that your offering will include the things that those patrons will expect and want. Once you've answered those, there are several follow-up questions that are equally, if not more important.

"Don't cling too tightly to your definitions of what your bar should be."
—Eben Freeman, Cocktail Culinaria

Concerning the Market

Will this concept work in this city/town? Are there other similar concepts that are already in operation? How are they doing? Can the market sustain another? Don't take your own word for it.

It's easy to fall into the traps of confirmation bias when assessing the viability of a bar concept. Especially if it's your concept. Don't say to yourself: "I know this worked in _____ city/neighborhood, so I'm pretty sure it would work here." Or any number of other optimistic platitudes along those lines.

Try to figure out all of the possible reasons that a concept wouldn't work now. Now is a much better time to learn that it's a bad idea rather than after you've begun spending thousands of dollars.

Ask other people you know what they think of the idea. (And please don't fall into the misbegotten trap of trying to "guard" your idea, or not tell people, lest someone steal it. Ideas are cheap, execution is what really separates you in this business.) The greater the variety of viewpoints you can find the better—no matter how many you get, it probably still won't be as wide a sample set of opinions as those of your future customers.

Ask yourself: What area or neighborhood would be the best fit for this bar?

There's no perfect answer for how much detail you need to go into on the above questions. But a good rule of thumb is that if you're not sure whether you have a clear enough answer then you probably don't have a clear enough answer.

If you're in a smaller market, you may want the main focus to be on making the drinks program accessible and welcoming to a clientele not familiar with craft cocktails. In a larger market, with established and well-known cocktail programs, it will be harder to stand out and this will put more pressure on your marketing team and the leadership of your drinks program (both of which may be just you in the beginning, so plan accordingly!)

Bar Profile

Little Jack's Tavern

710 King St., Charleston, SC
www.littlejackstavern.com

Little Jack's is one of the most carefully considered concepts you'll find. The vibe is that of a vintage American tavern, and that feel is evident from the perfectly curved bench seat on the banquette just inside the door, to the efficient use of square feet, to the many vintage lighting fixtures—all of which work perfectly together. Anyone who has spent time in Little Jack's immediately understands that owner Brooks Reitz knows how to make a room feel welcoming.

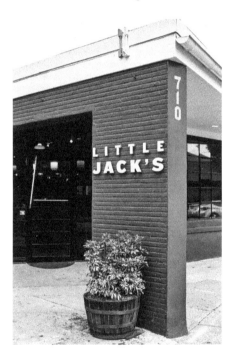

Little Jack's Tavern

Which Comes First, Location or Concept?

Planning the concept of your bar and choosing the location is a chicken or egg style conundrum. There are different ways to approach this. You can come up with a concept, and figure out what your ideal location would be and look until you find it. You could find a great location and assess the neighborhood and its needs, then design for what is missing from the area as well as what it will support.

Brooks Reitz, owner of Little Jack's and Leon's Oyster Shop in Charleston, has a solidly balanced approach to this. "I typically have several loose ideas for bar and restaurant concepts floating around in my head and then, once we've found a location that we feel like has promise, it's just a matter of figuring out which will be the best fit for what we're doing."

Regardless of how you approach it, your concept and location will be two of the main factors that determine the overall success of your business. So don't rush this part of the process. It may seem daunting, but that's okay.

"Start with your strengths" is the advice of Charlie Hodge, who has led the opening of 14 bars, including the famous Clyde Common in Portland, and now owns Sovereign Remedies in Asheville, NC. Begin with what you are most sure about, and expand your ideas outward from there.

Perhaps the most important thing to remember about this part of the process is to be flexible. Your concept or location (or both) may dictate changes to your plans, so be prepared for that. Erick Castro of Polite Provisions put it bluntly, saying: "Don't be married to one concept."

Max Poppel and Dan Rose, owners of The Flying Squirrel in Chattanooga agreed, saying they felt their bar had to actually be open before they were able to fully complete the concept.

A Brief Note on Naming

Now is a good time to discuss the subject of naming the bar. If you already have a name in mind for your bar, that's great. If you don't, well, we've all been there. In my experience naming a company or business either happens quickly and easily or is a long, difficult slog. Either way, the sooner you have a name the better.

Once you have a name in mind, it is extremely important to get it trademarked. Even if you're just planning on having a little bar in a small town, it is still crucial to trademark the name of the business. Chances are that the trademark fee will be far less than the cost of new signage, branding, menus and advertising if you were forced to change your name later.

In fact, I know of more than one place that has received a cease and desist letter from a lawyer representing the owners of a trademark they had infringed (unknowingly, in most cases). And in every single one of those instances the business had to do an expensive re-branding. It's worth taking the extra time to avoid letting it happen to you.

If you're in the US you can do a quick online trademark search on trademarkia.com or on uspto.gov to help rule out obviously trademarked candidates. (Other countries vary greatly, so check your government website.) Once you've settled on a name and done some initial research to make sure that no one else is using it in the industry, it's important to involve an attorney or engage a trademarking service on your behalf. Just because it doesn't show up in a basic search, or isn't in use within the industry, doesn't necessarily mean that it won't infringe upon someone else's mark. Don't let yourself think that you can skip this step.

A Brief Note On Money

In the next section we will talk more about projections and pro-formas, but before you get too far down the path of planning, make sure you have (or have access to) way more money than whatever you think you will need.

Bars are expensive to open. On the very low end you're looking at low six figures, but depending on the buildout costs, square footage, style, and numerous other factors, opening a bar can often cost several times that, or even into the millions in larger metropolitan markets.

> **"Be honest with yourself: are you capitalized enough to get through your first year?"**
> —Andrew Friedman, Liberty, Seattle

And those are just the opening costs—it's absolutely critical to have operating capital on-hand at opening. The general wisdom in the industry is to have at least six months of operating costs on hand. If the place is a smashing success from day one and you never have to touch a dime of these funds that's great, but it is too risky not to have it.

Sadly, I know numerous stories of bars and restaurants that had to close within months of opening because they were undercapitalized for operating. Some of those places might have become profitable and successful if they'd just had a little more runway. Don't let that happen to you.

We will come back to this subject later, but for now, just remember: The total costs will likely be higher than anything that's in your head at this point. Thinking about additional funding possibilities couldn't be a bad thing to do.

It's also worth noting, that several of the successful operators I spoke with talked about having to pivot after being open for a while, because one element or another of their concept wasn't working. These were experienced owners who knew most of the stuff in this book inside and out, and yet they still misjudged what the clientele would want.

There are no crystal balls that tell you exactly what will fit in a given area. When things do need to be adjusted, it takes money to do it. And when things need to be adjusted it also means they aren't going as well as you would've liked, so you've already had more money going out and less coming in than planned. This is why it's important to have six months of working capital on hand.

It should be noted too, that when I say six months of working capital, that is to say your *total costs to operate at expected levels of business*. That means all of your fixed costs (rent, insurance, etc), all of your labor costs (management, bar staff, kitchen staff, floor staff, yourself, etc) and all of your cost of goods (liquor purchases, food purchases, beer, wine, etc). This number often turns out to be a good bit bigger than you suspect.

Partnerships: Joy, Discontent & More

If you are planning on being a solo owner/operator, this section may not have much to offer. But with an industry as varied, involved, capital-intensive, and with so many elements that require oversight and management, many people choose to enter into partnerships.

A business partnership, much like a marriage, is whatever you make of it. If you put the work in, commit to getting through the difficult times, to working through differences, and being clear, direct and open, amazing things can be accomplished. But it can just as easily fizzle out if one party isn't as committed to the partnership.

As Danny Shapiro, of Scofflaw and other bars in Chicago, said: "Everyone succumbs to emotion at some point." This is the main reason that it's important to figure out as many details as possible at the outset, before there are heightened emotions involved.

First and foremost: You should never enter into any business partnership without a formal Operating Agreement. This is a mistake I've seen many times, and made myself. The consequences can be severe, in terms of lost revenue, lost sleep, potential legal fees, broken relationships and hurt feelings.

An Operating Agreement should always be executed and approved by a lawyer. I know a very unfortunate story of partners in a successful bar who skipped this step. They had an Operating Agreement, but didn't bother to have it actually checked by a lawyer. After their relationship went south they eventually ended up in a court battle for control of the bar, and some improperly worded sections of their operating agreement were a key part of the case.

Don't let yourself think *"My partners and I get along great, and we're just so strapped for cash right now, we can skip this until later."* If you can't afford to have a properly executed

Operating Agreement then you can't afford to open the business. It's that simple.

Operating Agreements can vary substantially, but here are a few areas that you should be sure to cover in detail:

Decision Making

What happens when you disagree? This is the fundamental question, and it must be answered clearly, thoroughly, and to the satisfaction of all partners.

Clear Delineation of Roles

It is nearly impossible to have too much clarity in this area. Many of the best partnerships I've seen involve partners who have complementary skill sets and very clear ideas of who has the final say on what.

That doesn't mean that one doesn't listen to new ideas or differing opinions, but more that everyone acknowledges what falls into their area of responsibility and what falls into someone else's, and respects each other's decisions, even if they disagree.

What If One of You Quits?

If one partner gets a lucrative job offer and takes it, or just walks out because of a severe disagreement, do they still receive a share of ongoing profits? Do they still have decision-making or voting power?

Trust me, this is not something you want to be trying to figure out in the middle of a tense situation. It didn't work out well for me the time I entered into a partnership without a clear Operating Agreement, and I've known many others who have also learned this lesson the hard way.

Cash Calls

Let's say it's six months in, and the three partners believe in the business, but it hasn't gotten into the black yet.

The business needs $60,000 in operating capital for the next few months before the tourist season comes. Partners A and B both put up $20,000 each, but partner C doesn't have the money. Partners A and B have the additional capital on hand and put it into the business. What happens? Does partner C's ownership % go down?

A good operating agreement spells out this type of situation (and others) in detail, and is approved by all members long before the actual difficult situation arises.

Death

If your business partner dies in a tragic accident does that mean their spouse, who may know nothing about the business, assumes their control and decision-making in the business? This is not a fun thing to talk about, but, once again, it should be spelled out, in the case that something unfortunate happens.

Exit Strategies

Let's say someone wants to buy your business and there isn't agreement about whether to take the offer. Or perhaps the business is doing well but one of you wants to sell your stake for one reason or another. Or a partner is forced to sell their ownership interest due to a divorce settlement.

The main thing here is to have a very clear set of steps laid out stating what will happen if a partner wants to leave the partnership.

On Design & Service Structure

There are numerous ways to approach the structure of service, but all of them fall somewhere on a scale. At one end, there is order-at-the-bar service. It's straightforward, simple and makes calculating your labor costs (and controlling them) simple. At the other end is full-service. A host (or two, sometimes), perhaps a coat check, and personalized and attentive service for every seat in the house.

If you want your bar to have a divey feel, you may be able to get away with bar service only. On the other hand, if you're opening a high end place with an elevated price point, your clientele may not take kindly to having to make their way over to the bar every time they need a water refill or want to order another drink.

It's very important to understand what your service structure will be, because it will have an immense effect on the square footage needed to pull off the concept.

There is no correct or one-size-fits-all answer to the question of how to structure service. I've been to many great bars that were at one or the other end of that spectrum, and many great bars that were somewhere in between. What's important is to make sure that what you want to do makes sense and is congruent with the type of place that you want to open. It's very important to understand what your service structure will be, because it will have an immense effect on the square footage needed to pull off the concept. Here are some key decisions that will dictate what you will need from a potential space.

How Will People Order?

First and foremost, will there be table service or not? If there is table service then there are numerous support stations (water, POS, dishes and silverware tubs, etc) that will need to be located throughout the room.

How Will People Enter & Sit Down?

Will there be a host seating people, a door person checking licenses, or will it be a communal, pub-type atmosphere where people find their own seats?

What happens when every seat is taken—are people allowed to stand?

Will There Be Food?

And, if there is, what type and how much? In many states bars are required to serve food in order to obtain an alcohol license. It's important to understand how the alcohol laws pertain to you. Sometimes they can have serious effects on the feasibility of a concept, or location.

The costs of building out a kitchen, and of the equipment required, are some of the most expensive per-square-foot of any bar or restaurant buildout. It's very difficult to gauge the level of food program that is best suited to a concept, so spend as much time on this as possible.

It's always good to have a couple of loose 'plan b's in place. One plan b if the demand for food is higher and you need to increase your food offering, and another plan b if the demand for food is lower than you expect and you need

Bar Profile
The Belmont

Charleston, SC

This is a fantastic example of a classic, small, efficient bar. The layout is set up perfectly for the business model, which features counter service and a very minimal food offering. Owner Mickey Moran, an experienced barman, worked with architect David Thompson to design the space, and it allows two bartenders to serve a full bar of people smoothly.

The centrally located bar allows a bartender to easily see the entire room without moving. The Belmont has a classic art-deco feel, which is enhanced by the uniquely shaped banquettes that cover the entire right side of the room, and the entrance, which echoes the same shape.

1 - Each bartender station is equipped with a bar sink, and ice bin. Fresh ingredients are kept inside each ice bin, in a sub-container.

2 - Equipment that must be shared by the two bartenders (glass washer and racks, undercounter freezer), is centrally located between the stations, accessible by either bartender.

3 - This area houses an espresso machine, deli slicer, and a couple of other smaller pieces of kitchen equipment. On slower nights the food menu (focused on charcuterie and cheese plates and homemade pop-tarts) is prepared by the bartenders, on busier nights by a barback.

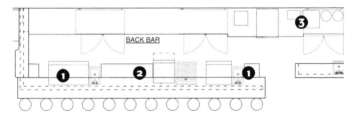

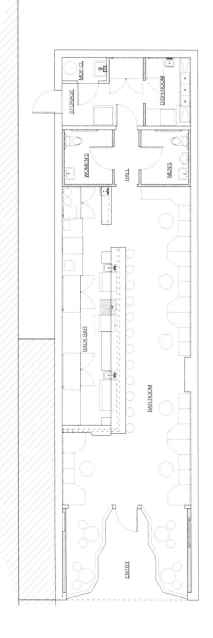

to scale it back in order to save on labor or food costs (or, plan for both).

A Brief Note On Standards of Service

No matter your approach to service, it is of immense importance that it be clearly defined for yourself and your employees. How little or much detail your standards of service have is up to you, but what's important is that it is understood and can be clearly communicated to staff.

Some common areas that should be addressed in your standards of service.

Greeting

When a new guest enters the bar, who greets them? How long should it take a staff member to greet a new arrival? Maybe there's a host, or a server who is in charge of greeting, or maybe it's the bartenders. Regardless of who on staff is responsible, it's important to be clear about it, so they know and you can observe if they're doing it well enough.

Seating

This question was posed above, but it bears repeating, because it is the deciding element of a guest's first impression as they enter your bar. If you're trying to be classy, a dive, or somewhere in between how the guest gets their seat will go a long way toward setting that expectation.

Waiting

Once every seat has been taken, what happens to the next people who walk through the door? Maybe they order a drink from the bar and lean against a wall-mounted drink rail until a table opens. Or perhaps they are sent away to wait for a text or call when their seats are ready. Or maybe it's somewhere in between—but you must have a clear system.

Ordering

Once seated, is there table service or should the guest order at the bar? If they must order at the bar, should they wait there for their drinks, or are they brought over to their table once a tab is opened?

Mistakes

Good standards of service will also spell out what a bartender should do if they make the incorrect drink. Pour it out? Ring it onto a comp tab? Give it to someone sitting at the bar? It should also cover what staff should do when a guest doesn't like their drink or is unhappy with it.

Standards

It's also a good idea to let staff know what you expect them to do if they see another staff member sending out something that has been prepared incorrectly. Maybe it's a cocktail with the wrong garnish, or a salad that should have a different dressing—what do you want one of your employees to do when they see that?

Complaints

How should a complaint from a guest be handled? What is an employee authorized to do and what are they not authorized to do? In an age in which Yelp and TripAdvisor reviews can sometimes help determine the fate of a business, how complaints are handled is now more important than ever. I recommend having a clear written process, that spells out specific procedures for both in-person complaints and for responding to emails and reviews.

On Tools & Techniques For Effective Bartending

Having the right tools is important for any craftsperson, and it's no different for a bartender. Cocktail Kingdom (www.cocktailkingdom.com) is the standard go-to in the industry for bartending equipment, and they carry most of the other leading manufacturers as well. There are other good resources as well—just do your homework, use the tools yourself and make sure that what you're getting is of high and lasting quality.

Sure, you can go on Amazon and buy tools that look similar to those on Cocktail Kingdom, or other reputable manufacturers, but you'll also find that many of those cheaper ones on Amazon have serious drawbacks. I recently tested a nearly identical off-brand jigger against a high quality one from Cocktail Kingdom. They looked exactly the same, but the 2 oz rim on the off-brand was actually 2.18 oz. That may not seem like a lot at a glance, but when some of your higher-end spirits may sell for $20-30 per oz, it can add up to a pretty significant amount over time.

For the most thorough explication of the best techniques and tools of our trade look no further than *The Bar Book*, by Jeffrey Morgenthaler, who runs the famous Clyde Common in Portland, OR.

On Developing A Cocktail List

Balance is a word that usually comes up often when

you're developing a cocktail list. Achieving a good balance is important whether your cocktail list is broad, ambitious and novel in presentation, or simply a page that says "Cocktails" with eight or ten drinks listed below.

So what areas require 'balance'? Here are some of the main things to evaluate as you put a cocktail menu together.

Base Spirits
It's necessary to make sure the core spirit groups of whiskey, tequila, gin, vodka, rum and brandy are all represented. Depending on your concept you may want to also highlight different types of whiskey or tequila, lesser-known spirits like Aquavit or Sotol, or drinks with liqueur bases.

Preparation & Serving Style
Generally (and this is far from an inviolable rule) drinks that feature citrus juice are shaken and those that don't are stirred. Stirred drinks will often tend to be more spirit-forward and have less dilution.

There are many other styles of drink preparation, such as swizzles or fizzes, and there are many great drinks in every category. But, sadly, it is a fact of bar life that many patrons will only look for a shaken drink that's served up, or others only want something that comes on the rocks. If your list does not represent a broad enough style of drinks, a portion of your customers will invariably leave disappointed.

ABV
For various reasons, both practical and legal, it's good to make sure that your drinks selection isn't tilted too heavily towards drinks that are high in alcohol content.

Ingredient Cross-Utilization

Let's say you sell a ton of Old Fashioneds and go through cases of oranges to garnish them. That's great...but if you're then throwing out lots of oranges post-garnish then that also is inefficient utilization. In this case a drink that uses orange juice should be added to the cocktail menu.

Or, let's say you have a great cocktail list, but there are different ingredients in every drink—the bartender will have to keep so many bottles on hand that their station may be too cluttered.

It also means that they likely won't be able to build multiple drinks using the same bottle, which will add crucial seconds to every large order.

Price

Some bars make it a feature of their menu to have line pricing, with all drinks at the same amount. If you don't take that approach, it's good to make sure that there is a fair spread across your desired price range.

Number of Steps

The Ramos Gin Fizz is a delicious classic drink, as is the Manhattan. But there's no question which of those drinks a bartender would rather receive an order for during a busy time, because the Ramos takes 3-4 times as long (or more) to make.

When developing a list, it's important to make sure that labor intensive drinks are not overly represented.

The main thing to keep in mind when creating a cocktail list, to quote Brooks Reitz of Little Jack's and Leon's in Charleston, is that "the drink menu has to be conceptually correct for the place."

Pricing A Cocktail List

The mechanics of pricing a cocktail list are quite straightforward, but still something that many new owners struggle with. There are several reasons for this. First and foremost, it requires time, focus and actually doing some math. Second is that there are a number of costs that can get overlooked, which can add up significantly over time. Let's start with pour cost. (Note: there's a downloadable spreadsheet of this available at www.cocktailbarbook.com.)

Here is a table showing the calculations for the pour cost of a classic drink from the 1920's, the Boulevardier.

INGREDIENT	AMT.	COST	NOTES
Jim Beam 4 yr	1 oz	.86	Bottle Cost (Jim Beam: $20.40) / Bottle Oz (25.5) = Per Oz Price (.86) * Amount (1.0)
Campari	1 oz	1.40	
Dolin Sweet Vermouth	1 oz	.55	
Total Pour Cost		$2.81	

This is a pretty straightforward drink, when it comes to the cost of the ingredients (which can vary greatly from one market to another). But there are the other ancillary costs to consider.

· Napkins/Coasters
· Garnish
· Dishwashing Costs
· Glassware Replacement Costs
· Ingredient Prep Labor Costs

Likely each of the above areas will be somewhere between $0.005 - $0.07 each, (some may even be less than half a penny per drink) when you do all the math based on your operations. It may not seem like much per se, but when you multiply it by tens of thousands of drinks per year it can become a meaningful amount of money fairly quickly. Add these costs to your pour cost to get total drink cost. Then (as in the table below) divide your total drink cost by your proposed menu price to get your cost percentage.

BOULEVARDIER	
Pour Cost:	2.81
Ancillary Costs:	0.07
Total Drink Cost:	$2.88
Proposed Menu Price:	$12
Cost Percentage	24.0%

This should be done for *every* drink on your menu, as well as for every drink that isn't on the menu but may be sold with regularity, or put on special. If you feature price-based specials, there's a significant extra amount of math involved, because you must ensure you receive enough additional customers from the special to justify the price reduction.

The costing out of specials is, in my experience, a much more involved process than most people realize or expect. In the interest of space, I'll forego pasting in the tables of numbers necessary for pricing out specials. If that is something you are interested in doing, I've provided a download-able spreadsheet on the book website.

Additional Thoughts on Pricing

Despite it being a fairly straightforward process, proper pricing is one of the things many bars and restaurants fall short on. As mentioned before, pricing and required margins vary greatly from one market to the next, but no matter where you are nothing can damage the bottom line quicker than improper margins. Here are a few general tips.

Regular Review of Margins

It's one thing to have everything on your menu properly costed, but that alone doesn't ensure that your margins will stay at the proper level. Prices change. Bartenders (and their amount of care and spillage) change.

Keg Yields

Look at your keg yields closely when you look through your detailed sales reports. A poorly maintained draft system can lead to excessive foam, and lost profits.

Food Costs

I have seen many bars and restaurants struggle to get food costs under control at one time or another.

There are many moving parts to proper food costing (recipes, effective portion control, prep labor, etc), and it's another one of those areas where it's absolutely key to have someone who has experience doing it and getting it right.

If that's not you, then I urge you to find someone who fits the bill.

A Few Words About Culture & Why It's the Main Indicator of Long-Term Success

Bars always change and evolve over time. There's turnover among staff, rearrangement of furniture or remodeling of the space, and changes in menu focus and style.

Some bars refine and improve over time, others deliver disappointing experiences to guests and little by little (or sometimes quickly) traffic drops off, and eventually a For Rent sign is hanging in the window.

Getting any brick and mortar business open is an accomplishment for an entrepreneur. Opening a bar, with the numerous bureaucratic, legal and logistical hurdles one must navigate, is quite the feat.

Sadly though, many of these businesses don't make it out of their adolescence and become long-term successes. As I spoke to bar owners across the country for this book, one of the most common factors that came up when discussing the longevity and long-term success of a business was its culture.

Other writers have written on the subject of how to go about creating a great culture. (See cocktailbarbook. com for a few book recommendations and a template of the document described in the next section.) Yet despite the wealth of advice available, it still remains elusive to many organizations.

Surely one of the reasons for this is that culture is a fairly nebulous, indefinable thing. Either you have it, or you don't, as the old saying goes. It lacks the standard metrics that people love to use to evaluate companies. It doesn't show a definitive percent change from one year to the next. It doesn't have solid Key Performance Indicators that can be matched to revenue. Nonetheless, it's now universally recognized as a key component of long-term success.

It should also be said that many people dismiss the idea of focusing and working on a culture as too touchy-feely, or more commonly, something that should be done later, when the company is bigger. I've heard people say those exact things in the past—and in nearly every case their companies had some seriously dysfunctional issues.

You could spend an entire career trying to figure out how to create a great culture and still not figure it out. That said, here's a brief list of some things that I've seen help people establish a successful, excited and dynamic culture within their company.

Have a Central Goal

Your Central Goal could also be described as your core long-term objective for the business. Maybe it's to become the best cocktail bar in your town, or be known for high-level drinks and the best service in the area.

The key is to define what the Central Goal is so it can be communicated to the rest of your organization. Then, define what will be necessary to make the Central Goal happen.

Here's an example—*To create an atmosphere of luxury and attentive service, combined with extraordinary craft cocktails that are inspired by Japanese drinking culture.*

Define the Habits Necessary to the Goal

Once you have a goal, your habits as an organization are what will move you toward (or away) from that goal. The habits that will be most important for your business' success could involve refining and examining service standards. They might address communication, or how employees treat each other. Or, they may regard specific areas of knowledge and focus within the cocktail or spirits programs.

The important thing is that these habits are defined, and then referred to from time to time to ensure they are being utilized. Most of the time they won't be more than three or four bullet points.

Define the Values of the Company
Maybe it's to always put employees first, or maybe it's that quality should never be compromised—it all depends on your concept.

In my company we refer to our values whenever we're struggling with a decision, and it has always been helpful. Like the above this can usually be organized into a few bullet points.

Create Clarity
Once you have the goal, habits, and values of your company, the final step is to create clarity within the company about all of them. This is not something that can be checked off a list, because it must be continually reinforced on an ongoing basis.

The best suggestion I have for you is to constantly model these things for your staff, and continually point out how various behaviors, practices, and methods support them.

Having solid communication and accountability systems does a large part of creating clarity within your organization. The makeup of those systems within your company might include technology solutions like Slack or Basecamp, or rely more on face to face meetings.

In either case though, the end result of everyone being on the same page is a common element among nearly all top bar programs (and many top companies in general).

The point of these exercises isn't just to have each bullet written out, but rather to create reference points to check against as future decisions are made. I can tell you from experience, once you're in the day-to-day muck of staffing issues, equipment or building problems, or any one of a million other things, it's not always easy to achieve the perspective to make sure that each decision is the best long-term choice for your business. Having these as a reference point can be a great help.

As mentioned above, a large portion of the operators I spoke to felt that creating and maintaining a culture was the most important ingredient to long-term success. I couldn't agree with them more. The costs (both real and in subtle incalculable ways) of having a poor culture, drag down many many businesses and keep them from being the flourishing companies they could be.

On These Things We've Covered

At this point, if you're working through everything in the book, you should have:

✔ A clear concept, defined in great detail, including both service structure and standards.

✔ Supporting research that the concept will work in your market.

✔ A name, or are working on it.

✔ Ideas for potential funding sources,

if necessary.

✔ An idea of what goes into effective cocktail list development and pricing, and bartending.

✔ An operating agreement, if going into business with partners.

✔ An idea of what the main focus and goal of your business will be, and how you'll go about achieving it.

✔ Basically, you have a clear idea of your concept, and have spent a good deal of time doing research that has helped you become confident that it will work in your market.

Onward!

PLANNING

[PART TWO]

business plans & their importance, location selection,
profile of Trick Dog, financial projections, start-up costs, breakeven,
estimating sales, architects and contractors, design, backbars, lighting

Something About Rubber & The Road

If the last section was all about what your bar will be, then this section is about figuring out the *how*. The number one thing that anyone who is evaluating your business— whether they're an investor, a potential partner, a bank, a mentor, etc—will want to see is a business plan.

A business plan is not optional, but the good news is that there are many helpful options now available to help, if you aren't familiar with writing one. I prefer to use liveplan.com, but there are many paid software options or even free templates available online. (The old adage that you get what you pay for certainly applies to many of the free business plan templates I've seen though.)

Many of the things we cover in this book will end up being part of your business plan, but taken as a whole they still don't obviate the need for one.

Location, Location, Location

Once you've determined that your business model is viable, the next step is finding a location. I recommend being absolutely ruthless in grading locations. Don't allow yourself to be blinded to a location's deficiencies because it has one particular aspect that you love. The idea of a "perfect" location that is well-priced, simple, easy to turn into a bar and has just the right amount of pedestrian traffic is great, but rarely a reality.

Some operators found their location almost immediately, others spent literally years looking for a space that was just right for the needs of their concept. Looking at real estate is another part of the process where it's important to keep an open mind and be flexible. When you begin to seriously consider a property dig as deeply as you can into these areas to make sure it's the right fit.

Why Wouldn't It Work Here?

Make a list of reasons why your business might not work in this particular location. This list should be as exhaustive as possible. There's a great chance that everything on the list will be counteracted by other factors, but you don't want to miss anything at this stage that will have an effect on your feasibility.

Traffic Levels

If the potential location is more of a commuter area, is there high enough visibility from the road? If you're in a downtown area, what is the foot traffic like? Will it be more than sufficient to justify the price of its rent?

Parking

Is there enough parking in the vicinity of the bar to accommodate your guests? Take the number of people you expect would be in the bar at capacity, and make sure there are enough spaces to accommodate at least half that number of cars.

Zoning

Zoning laws vary widely from one municipality to another, and many of them don't allow establishments that serve alcohol in certain areas. Before you get excited about a location be certain that it is zoned for your intended use.

Exterior Ambiance

Are the streetlights in the area in good repair? How are the sidewalks? The feel of the surrounding neighborhood has a large effect on a guest's first impression (and sometimes their willingness to visit in the first place).

Other Bars & Restaurants in the Area

Are there lots of other bars and restaurants nearby? Generally, the biggest key here is to make sure that your concept stands out and brings something new and unique to the area.

That new and unique thing also needs to be something that will appeal to the demographics that live in and visit the neighborhood.

Building Condition & Scope of Upfit

How old is the building? Upgrades to plumbing, electrical and HVAC systems on older buildings can get expensive very quickly. Having a rough idea of the scope of the upfit, and whether it will work within your budget is key.

___

A Brief Note on Assessing Locations

Over the years, I've heard many horror stories about prospective bar owners signing leases and spending money on building out a space, only to run into unexpected roadblocks later. I know one owner who leased a space, and went all the way through completing construction before learning about an obscure restriction that prevented him from serving alcohol in the location. These kinds of horror stories do actually happen.

Additional hours spent assessing potential issues at this early phase can potentially save lots of time, headaches and money later. Here are a few things that can help.

Talk to Your State Alcoholic Beverage Commission

This is a good first step, before investing too much time or money. Find out what is required from a license perspective, and make sure you are eligible.

Learn any location requirements that the state may require (For example, some states require bars serving liquor to have a full kitchen, or have a certain % of sales be from food.)

Architectural Feasibility Study

This is a service that most architecture firms offer and will typically cost $500-$1500, depending on the market and scope of the survey.

It's important to choose an architecture firm that has experience working with bars and restaurants and is familiar with all of the local zoning laws and how they relate to alcohol. Think of this (and the cost) as similar to getting an inspection on a house you're considering buying.

Budgeting & Pro-Formas

I once had a consulting client who was developing an idea for a classy pub in a large metropolitan market. The client had already found a new construction location and done some very rough projections, but he had never opened or operated a bar before.

After working up some realistic estimates for the space it became clear that not only was the rent higher than what his concept could sustain, but he had underestimated opening and operating costs by several hundred thousand dollars.

The client ended up abandoning the project altogether—just before he committed to signing a lease on the space. Moral of the story: Be sure that the numbers will work for a space before you sign anything binding.

"It's about absolute due diligence, especially with regard to the [building and alcohol] codes."

—Charlie Hodge, Sovereign Remedies, Asheville, NC

A Brief Note on Financial Projections

Let's start with the obvious statement about pre-opening financial projections: they're all abstract conjecture. Saying your gross revenue for next October will be x is akin to saying what color the next bird that flies past will be.

So, that said, what is the point in doing them? Projections demonstrate that you understand the mechanics of the business. They show that you can forecast the ebb and flow of your business for different nights of the week, different seasons and special events, for example. Knowing the projections allows you to reflect those variables in the various other areas that might be affected, such as staffing costs.

Bar Profile

Trick Dog

3010 Twentieth St., San Francisco, CA, 94110
www.trickdogbar.com

Located in the Mission district of San Francisco, Trick Dog's converted warehouse space puts out world-class drinks in an eclectic space. Their deeply conceptual cocktail menus (a Pantone menu, a dog calendar, a children's book—just to name a few) are famous the world over, and the release of a new menu every six months has become an anticipated event in the San Francisco drinking community.

If you understand the underlying mechanics of the business you will be able to diagnose issues and inefficiencies, and identify opportunities to maximize your revenue. That's what any lending bank or investor is going to want to see, and it should be the standard you hold yourself to even if you don't need to seek outside funding.

Over the years I've done projections and pro-formas for a number of bars and restaurants. Some of them performed below what we'd hoped, some exceeded our projections and became very profitable. I've also put together a complete set of numbers for several bars that ended up never opening. In every instance though, the exercise was worth it, and the time spent on crunching these numbers well spent.

Getting to Know Start-Up Costs & Pro-Formas

Before finalizing a lease, you have to be absolutely sure that your sales projections align with the lease rate. In other words, at this point you need to spend some serious time on budgeting and pro-formas.

Don't let yourself fall in love with a space and decide that it's just what you want—only to figure out later that your concept won't provide the gross revenue to justify the lease and the upfit (or one of those, but not both). "Find the truth of your space, then make sure that the numbers work with that," was the way Sovereign Remedies' Charlie Hodge put it.

In other words, try to figure out the top end for how much your buildout will cost and the low-end for what your gross sales will be, then figure out if you can make that work. If you can't, then you need to rethink your risk tolerance, and how firmly you believe in the space you're considering.

In this industry there are businesses that gross $500,000 per year and lose money, and there are also those who gross $500,000 per year and have six figure profits. Those outcomes are shaped significantly by decisions made at this early stage of the game.

Some Finer Points of Estimating Start-Up Costs

The most difficult area of start-up costs to make estimations is construction—which also has the biggest margin for error. Here's a good basic rule of thumb: whatever your first guess is, it will cost more. Nearly always a lot more.

Even veterans of the business still often find themselves struggling to stay within budget during the build-out process. Here are a few keys to navigating this maze.

Don't Take Your Own Word For It

Sure, you built the bathroom in your garage apartment with just over $1100 and some elbow grease. That's not the way things work in a commercial setting.

For instance, the plumbing code in many areas specifies that restroom faucets be either metered or infrared, which translates to a cost of $300-400 per faucet, plus having them installed by a licensed plumber. That's just one example.

Those required aluminum grab bars next to the toilet? $50-100 each. There are many many little things like this—and they can add up in ways you never imagined.

Your architect will likely have relationships with contractors who can give you rough estimates (we cover the finer points of selecting a contractor later in this section).

The main thing though is that it's important to get a few professional opinions on the costs to take the prospective location from its current state to what you want it to be. Once you have that input, overestimate even more.

Overestimate Every Category
There will nearly inevitably be start-up cost categories that you don't consider. Maybe it's the cost of a sign permit, or additional landscaping that you didn't know would be required by code.

Maybe it's replacing a door because it doesn't swing in the proper direction. There's always something.

My approach to this is to try to estimate high in every category, add a budget line item for Misc. in each category, and then add 25% to the total project cost for overages.

Think of Monthly vs. Up-Front Costs
There are some things, such as dishwashers, or refrigeration equipment, that can be leased instead of purchased.

Sometimes shaving a few thousand dollars off your start-up costs can be much more important than raising your monthly fixed costs by a couple hundred dollars.

Figuring Out Your Breakeven
After you have a handle on start-up costs, next comes Profit & Loss Pro-Formas, and from that you can find your breakeven point. In its simplest form:

Breakeven is when Total Sales = Total Costs (Fixed Costs + Labor Costs + Cost of Goods Sold)

Knowing this number (and tracking as you go to see where you may have made assumptive errors) is crucial early in the life of the bar, and it's truly the first benchmark to strive for once the business is open.

Some Finer Points of Making P&L Pro-Formas

There are no hard and fast rules when it comes to creating revenue projections, but here are some general suggestions based on my experiences and career.

Rent/Gross Sales Ratio

A fairly common f&b industry metric is that your rent should be 4-8% of your gross sales.

There are certainly exceptions to that, depending on the real estate market or the business model. For some bars that don't serve food this ratio may be higher, but it's a good metric to know.

Labor Costs

It's not usually possible for one person to serve 100 customers, yet there are a lot of restaurant and bar business plans that have an expectation like this somewhere in their projections, once you look closely.

Let me put it succinctly: If you don't know what you're doing when it comes to estimating labor costs for your place, find someone who does.

Labor Costs Relative to Sales

Another common mistake that inexperienced owners make in projections (and something that savvy banks and lenders looking at an application from a restaurateur will look for) is large increases in sales that are not reflected in labor costs.

Overestimate Every Cost Category

There will invariably be costs that weren't in your projections. Maybe it's a $300 yearly HVAC service, a $60 monthly pest control, or the ongoing cost of buying glassware is higher than your think.

My approach to this is influenced directly by the quote below from one of my industry touchstones, Harry Johnson. I estimate each category as high as I can imagine it being, then add a line item for Misc. in each section of the pro-forma. This may sound familiar, from the Start-Up costs, and it's not a point that can be repeated too much.

Your business will constantly come up with creative new needs for money — one of the biggest keys to long-term success is the careful management of your expenses and expense and revenue projections.

"The chief point is to be liberal in the allowance for expenses, and there is then the possibility of greater profits than were expected."

—Harry Johnson, *Harry Johnson's Bartenders Manual* (1882)

Estimating Sales

There are nearly as many different ways of making sales projections as there are types of bars. For example purposes here we will use a fairly straightforward method. It's also worth mentioning that there are a plethora of business plan software programs available that have very straightforward and user-friendly systems for making and manipulating sales estimates. They can be helpful and time-saving if this isn't one of your areas of expertise.

As you'll see in the following chart, we'll first calculate how many customers are expected per day, and the check average. From there we can extrapolate total sales per day, week, month and year.

When making projections like this it is key to make appropriate adjustments for seasonal demand, based on your market. I would also recommend estimating sales for each day. Our example here shows one amount for weekdays and another for weekend nights, in the interest of clarity.

	WEEKDAY (SU-THU)	WEEKEND (FR-SA)
Customers Per Day	50	84
Average Check	$24.00	$30.00
Total Nightly Sales	$1,200	$2,520

This example also does not show seasonal fluctuation, since that varies widely from one market to the next. That should definitely be a consideration as you make your own projections. If you're planning to seek funding from a bank it will be one of the first things they look at as they go through your pro-formas.

From those estimates we can extrapolate monthly and annual totals. Using the above assumption, our sales would be as follows:

Total Weekly Sales	$11,040
Total Monthly Sales	$47,480
Total Annual Sales	$574,080

Now these numbers can be compared to your cost estimates to begin to get an idea of the volume that will be necessary for the business to sustain itself. Like many things in this business, making P&L pro-formas is not something that should be blundered through wantonly.

When I look back at some of my first pro-formas I cringe, and would be loathe to show them to anyone. They had so little bearing on the realities of what the business ended up being that it's almost funny.

If you haven't done this before, do yourself the favor of finding someone with experience to give you some tips and look over your initial efforts. This might be an accountant, a consultant, or an experienced owner, but any attached costs will definitely pay for themselves in the long run.

Final Thoughts on Pro-Formas

See cocktailbarbook.com for a downloadable template of an annual Profit & Loss Pro-Forma. For the sake of space we haven't included a more detailed breakdown here, but just remember that this is one of the most critical things you will do for your business, and how well you do it will go a long way toward dictating your success or failure.

It should also be noted that pro-formas should not be discarded to the junk heap (or archive folder) of start-up files. Ideally, they are living documents that are referred to, adjusted, and referenced on an ongoing basis. In my businesses we review our pro-formas on a monthly basis, to make sure that each category is in alignment with our estimates. Anything that isn't in line is then examined and we adjust either our prices, processes, or estimates accordingly.

A Primer on Hiring Architects & Contractors

Finding the right architects and contractors can be the difference between a relatively smooth buildout and a nightmare, and can also make a tremendous difference to your bottom line. Designing for hospitality includes many particularities and unique requirements, so it's important that the firm you engage have familiarity with concepts similar to yours. Kenta Goto, owner of Bar Goto in NYC, recommended finding bars or restaurants that had design elements you like and then contacting the architects of those spaces.

Unfortunately, as with many things, there's no guaranteed way to make sure that you're finding the right person. That said, here are a few guidelines that should be helpful.

Industry Examples

Look at examples of other projects the architect or contractor has done in the industry. Ask how well the process was for both them and the owner. Did the project stay on budget? Are there any of their clients in the industry that you could speak to, and ask about their experience?

Other Operators

Ask other restaurant or bar owners in your market who their architects and general contractors were. Were they happy with the process?

Do You Like Each Other?

Do you get along easily with the prospective hire and have a natural rapport? The value of your personal connection is easy to underestimate, but considering you will be going through a stressful experience together, it can also be quite important.

This isn't a choice to be rushed. I recommend getting quotes from at least 2-3 firms. Compare and contrast the quotes carefully—sometimes the services provided from one quote to another can vary widely.

Those same keystones for selecting an architect apply when choosing a general contractor. Construction costs (and contractor markups, which are commonly called P&O, for pricing and overhead) can vary widely from one market to another, and one type of project to another. Chances are, your architect may be able to recommend a GC or two that they have previously worked with. Even so, it's still important to get multiple quotes for the sake of comparison. Many architects will also provide the service of helping evaluate construction quotes.

On Branding & Graphic Design

After you've chosen a name you'll need a graphic designer to create a branding package, menus and other elements that comprise the graphic identity of the bar. As with selecting contractors, architects, and other types of contract hires, one of the best ways to find people who will be a good fit is to find designs you like, find out who designed them and then contact that person.

Having done this a number of times, it's always interesting to see the range of quotes you can receive. I once sent out a request for proposal for a fairly straightforward branding package and received quotes that ranged from $8,000 - $50,000, and one company that politely said "if you have to ask..." Here are a few keys you'll be looking for when working with a graphic design professional.

Style Guide
This is a standard accompaniment to every logo and branding package. It has the logo, including whatever treatments, backgrounds, colors, and fonts were used.

A style guide also spells out appropriate font pairings, and what colors should be used in the branding.

Scope of Quote
Is menu design included in the initial quote from the designer, or is it something that will cost extra? If you aren't sure whether or something is part of a quote it should be clarified with the designer before the contract is signed.

Ongoing Costs
Unless you happen to be a graphic designer, or have one as a partner, you will almost certainly have ongoing design needs that will need to be filled by someone outside the company.

It's good to ascertain early in your relationship with a designer whether their rates will be compatible with your ongoing budgets and needs.

Some Bar & Restaurant Design Basics
There are a number of design standards in the bar industry, and deviating from them should only be done with caution, and a very good reason. Standard bar height is 42" off the floor. That doesn't mean yours necessarily has to be that height, but most backbar equipment (refrigerators, beer coolers, ice wells, glass chillers, etc) is designed to go under a 42" bar.

The outside of the bar, where people sit, is called the front bar. The sections behind the bartender as they face the guest are the backbar, nearly always the location of the liquor shelving. The sections underneath that house equipment, service wells, ice bins, and any number of other things are known as the underbar.

Typically, a bartop should extend 12" to 14" from its front wall to accommodate the legs of the patrons while they sit. They should overhang about the same amount from the backside of the wall, in order to partially cover backbar equipment and allow bartenders to reach across the bar comfortably. Here are a few other standards of note.

Barstools

You should count on 24" of width for each bar stool around a bar. This leaves appropriate space for most stools, and for guests to get in and out. If you have exceptionally bulky stools it may be necessary to budget a few additional inches per stool.

Table Height & Size

Standard table height is 30", and counter height tables are 36". Table sizes vary, and can be made to size. Generally, you should also budget at least 24" per seat, as with a barstool. If you're seating patrons on all four sides of a square table, 36" x 36" is the standard. A standard two person table is 24" x 30".

Passing Space

Anything less than 36" in a backbar space or on a kitchen line will likely be uncomfortably close for staff to pass each other (and probably not up to what is required by the build-ing codes).

Wider Main Pathways Are More Comfortable
Yes, code says that you only need a 36" wide walkway between those two tables. But if it is a pathway that will be heavily traveled (such as to a restroom or kitchen) a few extra inches will greatly enhance the experience of guests sitting at the tables in question.

These guidelines can at least get you started toward figuring out a seating plan for a space, and a design profes-sional can hone them in, or suggest others in order to truly make it work.

A Space Becomes a Bar
Once you've settled on a location, and made sure that the numbers can work, both in terms of capitalization and revenue, it's time to turn the location into a bar. This is one of the most fun and exciting parts of the business for many people.

Below are a few design elements to pay attention to as you go about assessing different potential layouts.

Energy Centers
This term refers to the parts of the space that naturally have a focus. The bar is your main energy center, but it could also be a communal table, a lounge area, or specific section of seating.

Unpopular Seating Areas
Most rooms will naturally have a couple of seating options

that are less desirable than other parts of the bar. It's important to acknowledge and identify them, and take measures to make the areas more welcoming to guests.

Congestion

What spaces are most likely to cause traffic congestion on a busy night? If there's a host, is there ample room for guests to wait when the host is occupied? Is a restroom located right across from the kitchen doors, causing traffic flow issues?

"[Creating a bar] is about channeling the intangibles, to create something unique."

—Josh Harris, Trick Dog, San Francisco

It's better to try and address things like this ahead of time than after you're open and getting complaints from guests about them.

Travel Distance

Are there any travel distances (between kitchen and dining room, or behind the bar, or from the bar to storage) that will become a problem when the place is busy?

If so, try and ascertain if there's a way to address them.

Storage Space

Where will the storage space be? Will it be sufficient? It's necessary to refer to your pro-formas. Sales volume (and delivery schedules) will dictate how much back-up inven-

What design element do you most often see bars get wrong?

"They don't pay enough attention to the energy centers of the bar."
—Josh Mazza, Seamstress, NYC

"The mechanics of the backbar design and layout."

"Spaces that are designed for busy weekends, not everyday business. The space needs to be comfortable even when it isn't packed."

"Backbar equipment layout."

"Lighting."

"Backbar ergonomics."

tory will need to be on-hand, which will in turn show how much square footage is needed for storage.

Defined Spaces
It doesn't take much for a room to feel good when it's full of happy customers having drinks together. On the other hand, some rooms feel uncomfortable and uninviting when they're anything less than half-full.

Bar Profile

Seamstress

339 E. 75th St. New York, NY, 10021
www.seamstressny.com

Tucked into the Upper East Side of NYC, Seamstress is a world-class bar in an unlikely location. The small, inviting space has two small bars, and a cozy, communal feel throughout. The layout is a great example of a design that creates comfortable flow between numerous seating areas, especially given the nontraditional footprint of the space. The variety of spaces also serve to give the bar a comfortable feel, at any time of evening or level of volume.

One of the most effective ways to avoid this particular misfortune is to have discrete spaces throughout your floor plan. Whether it's with booths, banquettes, a couch and chair seating area, or any number of other things, the key is to create areas as opposed to a room.

Many of these questions will have already been answered during the concepting process described in Section I, but it's usually time well spent to refer back through your notes and cross-reference each need with what the location offers. There are an immense amount of details that must work in concert together, and it's not hard to miss something here or there—I certainly have many times in my own bar designs.

Some Thoughts Specifically on Backbar Design

It's no coincidence that backbar design was overwhelmingly the frequent answer from bar owners about the most common mistake they see most bars make. Cocktail Culinaria principal Eben Freeman, formerly of Genuine Liquorette and wd-50, among others, stressed the point that even architects who have restaurant design experience are not usually familiar with the nuances required to do efficient cocktail service.

One of the most critical elements of bartending, whether you're slinging PBR in an indie rock club or making Mai-Tai's in a fancy tiki bar, is always speed. Craft cocktails are an extremely labor intensive endeavor. Even a simple drink can take a significant amount of time to prepare in an environment that isn't built to maximize speed, and any improvements that can be made to shave time (without sacrificing any quality) off that will mean a lot in the long run. In the Operations section we will talk about some of the steps you can take in day to day operations to be efficient, but the effects of a poorly laid out backbar will be felt for the entire life of the business.

That said, getting someone with significant bartending or backbar design experience to look at your plans with an eye toward efficiency can potentially have a huge effect on your bottom line later. Here are some important elements to consider as you work out your backbar design.

Stations

The area immediately surrounding a bartender as they are in position behind the bar is referred to as their station.

In an ideally designed bar station the bartender would be able to reach everything necessary to make any cocktails they can expect to be ordered with any frequency, without having to move either foot.

Think of everything that the bartender can reach within arm's length as a circle. Now think of a slightly larger circle: this represents everything a bartender can reach if they move one foot. This circle usually adds 18" on either side of the bartender, or 3' to the overall diameter of the circle. Anything that is not within this area represents something the bartender will have to take steps to reach, and could impact the speed of service.

Shared Equipment

Determine what pieces of equipment will have to be shared between your bartender stations, and then make sure that they are located in between each station.

It's also important to evaluate the placement of all

shared equipment from a traffic flow perspective. For instance, it's good to avoid placing two pieces of equipment that will often require staff to stop to use (a beer cooler and an undercounter wine fridge, for example) across from each other on the forward and rear underbar areas.

Poor placement of shared equipment inevitably just leads to traffic jams during busy times, which translate to lost time and money for the business. Seconds matter a lot when it comes to how long the ticket time is for each drink the bar serves.

Well Space
Once you know how many cocktails will be on your list you can then make an ingredient list and ascertain how many bottles each bartender will need to have at their fingertips.

Ideally, a bartender should be able to reach everything necessary to make all core drinks on the cocktail list without taking more than one step.

Trash Cans
To quote one of the owners I spoke to, "...even the industry big boys, with multi-million dollar buildouts, make mistakes and might forget something, like: where's the trashcan behind the bar?" I've made the very same mistake myself (though without the multi-million dollar budget).

The best advice I have is to just think through an evening of service, in as much detail as possible, and figure out what the needs of the staff will be, and how they're each solved within the area behind the bar. And, if possible, leave some extra empty space. There will always be a few things that need to find a place behind the bar that aren't thought of during the planning phase.

Dish Racks

If your dishwasher is located behind the bar you must also make sure you have ample space for clean and dirty dish racks. I've seen this step forgotten as well, and dish racks that measure 21"x21" and drip water while steaming aren't always the simplest thing to just squeeze in somewhere.

Bottle Shelving

You can count on bottle diameter working out to an average of about 4", for backbar display purposes. This means that an 8' shelf with bottles one-deep will hold about 24 bottles.

Equipment With Additional Space Needs

A self-contained beer 'kegerator' will require a CO_2 tank to pressurize the lines. Make sure you leave space for that.

In some areas the fire code may require that tank to be chained to a wall, or have a certain amount of space on either side, which should also be considered.

Lighting & Its Discontents

A number of people I spoke to mentioned lighting as one of the most common mistakes they see bars make. I can think of many conversations I've had with other owners over the years about the best lighting approaches, styles and solutions. There is no one-size-fits-all answer, because every space is unique.

How to light the room is very much an area where, unless you have significant expertise already, it's best to seek the opinion of a design professional.

Lighting is a great example of that thinking. Whether it is you or a designer making the choices, here are a few key things to take into account when making fixture and style choices.

"You have to let your professionals do their job...know when your input is needed, and when you need to get out of the way."
—Neal Bodenheimer, Cure and Cane & Table

Lighting by Area
What type of light does each area need? Maybe it's general area lighting from a chandelier, focused lighting from a pendant, or subtle mood lighting from a wall sconce. Every seating area is different, and so is the lighting required to make it feel welcoming.

Cohesive Fixture Choices
Does the overall feel of each lighting fixture match that of both the space and the concept? You're looking for some cohesion between the style of each fixture and the concept for the bar and how they both work with the physical space itself. It's a delicate balance, but when achieved is a key element in creating a space that makes guests feel comfortable. This is the type of design element that has no measurable aspect, in terms of guest satisfaction, but when done correctly can be

a huge factor in creating a bar that people want to visit over and over again.

Dimmers
As a general rule, it's important to have every light fixture in a bar or restaurant on a dimmer.

Types of Light Fixture
A pendant fixture with a small pin-spot bulb in it might illuminate a small cone of light over a table or area of the bar. A sconce may light its immediate surrounding area. A chandelier usually provides a general wash of lighting for a larger area.

In each case, the specific type, style and purpose of the fixture will be markedly different. What is important is to work with your designer to consider each area, both individually and as a cohesive whole, and make lighting choices that work for the space as a whole.

What Element(s) Should & Shouldn't be Highlighted
Perhaps you have a cool old ceiling with wooden rafters and lots of characters. Some subtle track or flood lighting can help people notice their character. Obversely, if your ceiling isn't visually appealing that can potentially be overcome simply with dark paint and careful downlighting.

Closing Thoughts on Ambiance
Whitechapel and Smuggler's Cove owner Martin Cate said eloquently that a bar operator should strive to "create memorable, interesting experiences" for their guests.

Creating memorable and interesting experiences

requires the effective execution of many many constituent elements. First is the staff, their approach to guests, service, interactions, and their ability to do their job quickly and efficiently. This subject was covered in the last section, and will be addressed again later in this section.

One of the questions I asked during interviews for this book concerned the most common interior design mistakes these owners saw when they went into other bars. Ambiance came up time and again, and a few specific things merited repeating here.

Music
If there aren't playlists that have been created specifically, then it's a good idea to at least have some general guidelines for staff regarding what should and shouldn't be played, and at what volume.

Lighting Levels
We've already covered lighting in detail, but even great light-

ing can make the room feel dreadful if set at an improper level of brightness.

Staff Mood

This might not be the first thing to come to mind when you think of ambiance, but think about the last time you were out and the host or bartender looked very annoyed—did the bar feel comfortable and welcoming in that moment?

This falls under the purview of Standards of Service, but it's worth mentioning here, because it really can make or break the ambiance of the bar.

On These Things We've Covered

At this point, if you're working through everything in the book, you should have, in addition to the work from the previous sections:

✔ A location, or are becoming familiar with objectively assessing them.

✔ Overall design of the bar.

✔ Ideas on lighting, ambiance and feel of the bar.

✔ Carefully designed backbar that will support the concept, even at volume.

✔ Projections for Start-Up Costs and Pro-Formas.

✔ A name, which is in the trademark process, as well as a start on the branding and design process

OPENING

A Few Words About The Buildout Process

First and foremost, it's important to do everything you can to maintain your own sanity during the opening process. Keep in mind that this part that will most likely take significantly longer than you project, and cost a lot more than you imagine. No matter how much of a buffer you feel like you may have built into your projections in those two categories, reality is nearly always slower and/or more expensive.

During our interview Josh Harris laughingly mentioned a major article calling Trick Dog the most anticipated bar opening in San Francisco for 2010. The bar opened in 2013.

One of the most accurate descriptions I've heard of the buildout process was this: On a regular basis throughout the process things will come up that might delay the project a week or two, or cost five, ten or twenty thousand dollars, or maybe even both. Most of these will come to nothing. A few will end up being an issue that will cost time, money, or both, to fix. And you have no way of knowing which are which. Have fun.

This may sound like a somewhat bleak viewpoint on this aspect of the process. I don't mean for it to—for some, myself included, it's one of the most exciting and thrilling parts of the whole process. I just want to establish a framework for how to approach it, because I've seen it literally push people to a breakdown.

If you have regular routines, such as going to the gym or doing yoga, try to stick to them. Do whatever you can to get a decent night's sleep. Take a couple hours or an afternoon to recharge every now and then. This is the shortest section in the book, but it's separated on its own for a reason: it lives in its own type of grueling time that has no exact analogue in the day-to-day life of either planning or operating a business.

To put it as simply as possible: do everything you can to be at your best during this phase, because there will be a steady stream of complications, problems, delays or unforeseen difficulties that will take focus and your best decision-making skills during buildout and pre-opening.

Some Notes on Hiring & Training

It's a common refrain among bar owners that anyone can be trained to make a great drink, but far fewer people can be trained how not to be a jerk. And it's very true. Ultimately, your staff has more control than anyone else on whether a guest has a positive or negative experience.

That can happen in a number of ways—they could get the guest's order wrong and not notice. They could respond poorly to a complaint. Or not notice if someone is obviously unhappy with their drink. Or maybe the guest has been waiting overly long to pay their bill and are now getting impatient and the bartender is chatting casually with someone at the other end of the bar. These are the types of interactions that you may never know about as an owner, but will certainly have a long-term effect on the business.

On the flip side, even the most junior member of your staff has the ability to take a normal interaction and create a repeat customer, or a great experience that won't be soon forgotten by the guest. As Erick Castro of Polite Provisions noted: "Don't overlook training for the non-bartender staff. The servers, door person, host—those are the first people your customers come into contact with." It is sage advice. The first and last impression are much more likely to linger than anything that happens in between.

Ultimately, your staff has more control than anyone else on whether a guest has a positive or negative experience.

Hiring isn't the easiest thing to address in a format like this, because so much of hiring is individual to the person, and the establishment. When conducting interviews for this book I heard time and again that the biggest key to effective staff hiring is creating a culture, and then making sure that your hires fit in with that culture.

But what does that really mean? Whether by accident or design every business will have a culture and an intricate series of internal politics. Knowing that, it's up to you as the owner to make sure that the culture within your company functions in a way that reflects the values that are important to you. For a more in-depth discussion creating a culture see the end of Part I of the Planning section.

A Primer on Hiring Staff
Staffing, especially with regard to making new hires, is an area in which I've seen many operators underestimate the potential negative ramifications of a poor or hasty decision.

What traits do your best employees share?

"Positive disposition."

"Follow-through."

"An immense sense of responsibility and pride in the business."

"Enthusiasm and obedience."

"They don't take themselves too seriously, but [they are] also serious enough."

Neal Dodenheimer, Cure/Cane & Table, New Orleans

The cost, both in real dollars (such as spirit tastings, menu tastings, training materials, uniforms, etc) and intangibles (such as your time, your staff's time, staff morale, etc) of a new hire not working out are in most cases much higher than you might think.

So what can you do to make effective hires? Sadly, as with many facets of this business, there's no one size fits all answer, but here are a few steps that can be helpful when assessing the quality of an applicant.

Do a Background Check

This is fairly straightforward. There are some free services online, but they aren't always reliable. There are also paid background check services that aren't very expensive.

This is a worthy cost, trust me. I know stories of people who have skipped this step and ended up in less than ideal public relations situations as a result.

Call Previous Employers

This step often gets skipped, and I'm not sure why. If you've just met someone and they made a great impression, well, that's fantastic.

But sitting down with someone when they're doing everything they can to make a favorable impression will not always give you as much information as talking to a manager who saw them day-in, day-out as they worked.

Call Their References

This step is also straightforward and also often gets skipped. Many people skip calling references because they think that all references will be positive and thus it will be a waste of time. This couldn't be farther from the truth, and they can always be informative.

I recommend asking questions that will give you a better picture of what the prospective employee is like. How well do the reference know the applicant? Are they punctual? Does the person have lots of friends? Are they on good terms with their former bosses?

You can learn a lot more about an applicant than you might think, if you ask questions that aren't expected.

Some Thoughts On Training New Hires

The approaches that I've seen for training new hires range from a couple of hours of instruction on the POS, a

Bar Profile

Cure

4905 Freret St., New Orleans, LA, 70115
www.curenola.com

Cure, located in, and part of the revitalization of the Uptown section of New Orleans, is one of the top bars in the country. They also represent one of the most cohesive bar teams in the country. Co-owner Neal Bodenheimer refers to the team as a collective, and that fact shows in the minimal turnover and consistently excellent offering of Cure.

printout of the house cocktail builds, and maybe a couple of hours oversight on the job, to in-depth multi-week training programs. As with many other things, you need to find the right approach for your bar.

While the processes I heard about in my interviews varied greatly, here are a few successful elements I came across.

Apprentice Model
Both Neal Bodenheimer of Cure, and Kala Brooks of Top of the Monk mentioned the importance in their bars of a defined apprentice-style system, where bartenders would first work as a barback, prior to becoming a bartender.

Benchmarks
If there are specific elements that are important to your cocktail program, then establish some benchmarks that staff must meet during training, and after. Maybe that's a list of core classics in addition to the regular menu, or familiarity with a certain style of whiskey. The key here is establishing clear expectations.

Clarity on Bar Standards
Several owners mentioned the importance of establishing the standards that are expected early (and consistently going forward), before bad habits could be learned or brought into the fold.

A Few Words On Accounting
Several of the operators I spoke with for this book mentioned the importance of starting with orderly and

correct accounting systems, and making sure that bookkeeping around the opening period doesn't fall behind. I've been on both sides of this, and it's far more expensive to have a professional go back and fix the numbers because they weren't set up correctly than it is to just do it right the first time. At a bare minimum, it's important to have an accountant examine the first two areas listed below.

"Money only comes in one way...and it goes out in many many ways."
—Josh Mazza, Seamstress, NYC

Start-Up Cost Categorization
Many of your start-up costs can be amortized over a period of years for accounting purposes, instead of just being a one-time cost. Not doing this correctly could mean thousands of dollars of differences in your tax burden.

Chart of Ongoing Accounts
Having all costs properly categorized is the only way to accurately find and diagnose any issues. Mistakes here can also easily lead to overpayment of taxes—or worse, underpayment and subsequent difficulties with the IRS.

Setting up proper systems that make sense for your business, and then keeping up with them is everything here. There are lots of spending areas that, unmonitored, can get out of control.

On These Things We've Covered
As mentioned at the beginning of the section (but

worth repeating) the build-out process is seldom smooth, easy, or inexpensive. It also does end eventually, and that's sometimes a good thing to remind yourself when you're in the middle of it, problems continually coming up and money continually going out.

At some point, seemingly (and perhaps literally) over-night you trade paint-stained work clothes for a button up shirt, and your hands are actually clean enough to shake those of your customers. And those customers are now coming in, marveling at the new bar that you've opened near their office, or only a few blocks from their house. There's a lot more to come, but it's well-deserved to take a few moments to savor the experience of getting open.

At this point you should have, in addition to the work from the previous sections:

✔ A bar
✔ A staff
✔ Lots of things to do every day

OPERATING

media, public relations, marketing, profile of Top of the Monk, waste, oversight, communication, ongoing training, inspections, systems and longevity

A nd here you are. The doors have just opened, customers are (hopefully) coming in. You're now a bar owner. Josh Harris of Trick Dog said that during their opening things were so hectic that when they opened for the first time (to a line of San Franciscans that stretched down the block, and had begun to assemble an hour before their 3:00 pm opening) they literally hadn't even finished putting the front door on. That finally happened a few hours before closing, late that night.

In my experience, the feelings following an opening are a mixture of excitement, exhaustion, relief, and fear. After all—you've just been through a brutal and trying experience, and yet now is when the real work starts, because now there's rent, distributor payments, payroll and all of the other aspects of day to day operations begging for your time and focus.

Neal Bodenheimer put it this way: "Don't try to do everything." He recounted how in the early days after Cure opened he would bartend, do the books, work on the cocktail list, print the menus and any number of other things, running himself ragged in the process. "My business partner finally said to me: You have to focus on the things you like."

Most bar operations are too big to be run well by just one person. Whatever the management structure of your place, it's a good idea to make sure that you aren't spreading yourself too thin, as well as to delegate where possible.

On Consistency & Quality Control

Consistency and quality do not come automatically, even if you've designed everything about the program well. These two areas take ongoing effort to sustain and improve upon, and should be treated accordingly.

Kala Brooks of Asheville, NC's Top of the Monk notes that she straw tests nearly every drink that goes across the bar to a customer whenever she is at the bar. It's important to remember that it's not necessarily about what you like, or what suits your palate. It's about making the drink to the spec that is correct for the bar, as Andrew Friedman of Liberty said.

Trying to set a standard of quality over time is a tall order, and the owners I spoke to approached it in a broad variety of ways. Here are a few things that have worked.

Clear Direction & Reinforcement

It's a fairly common mistake, especially in smaller markets, to see a new lead bartender or bar manager come in and then make a series of rapid changes to the program. Usually, this only serves to confuse regular patrons more than anything else. It's important to have a clear direction and focus for the bar, and how the drinks will be made and presented, that is communicated top-down throughout the organization.

Standard Builds

The importance of making sure your bartenders' drink recipes are standardized cannot be overstated. It might be an unhappy customer, whose Martini was great one week and lackluster the next.

Or it might be that a bartender pours an additional 1/4 oz. of whiskey into "their" Manhattan recipe, which over time can turn into thousands of dollars of lost profit for the bar. There are too many examples to list of the pratfalls that can be brought about by loose standards in this area. This was echoed again and again in my interviews. The bartenders should have the builds on-hand for all drinks on the menu, anything else that's popular with the clientele, and the house builds for all standard classics. Basically, anything that gets ordered more than once in a week should have a standardized build utilized by every bartender on staff.

"Let the drink speak for itself...your product should be your brand."

—Kenta Goto, Bar Goto, NYC

Testing Staff

As any manager knows, giving an employee access to information doesn't guarantee they will know it. Danny Shapiro of Scofflaw, among others, regularly gives his employees tests on the house builds for menu drinks and classics.

Andrew Friedman regularly has his entire staff at Liberty in Seattle make the same drink, at the same time, and then they pass around the results to taste as a group and detect whether any examples taste out of balance.

Leading by example is key here, as well as training all staff to take pride in putting out a drink of the proper quality. As Josh Mazza of Seamstress said, "The standard you walk past is the standard you accept...it has to be a broken windows policy [of not letting mistakes go]."

A Few Thoughts On Public Relations

If you have the goal of gaining media attention for your bar, I don't recommend trying to do it yourself, unless you have a background in marketing and public relations. Even if you do have a background in marketing and PR, it should still be approached with caution, because there are so many other things that will constantly pull at your time.

Whether you're doing it yourself, working with a freelancer, or hiring it out to a firm, here are a few general guidelines and tips.

Stay Ahead
Many magazines and other outlets work on a cycle several months out—or more. So plan accordingly, and make sure that you aren't pitching a story about your fall menu in September, as they're looking at New Year's stories.

Have A Plan
Consistent press coverage is not something that happens by accident, or by dint of the fact that you simply created a cool place. Bars that achieve results in this arena do so because they have a clear plan, and someone making it happen.

Don't Let Good Opportunities Go To Waste
This isn't the type of business where you will automatically have things that can be promoted and leveraged for press coverage. Sadly, it doesn't work to send out a press release

that says your drinks are just as good as they were last month, if not better. Thus, it's important to make the most of potential opportunities for promotion.

Launching a new menu? Make it into an event. Send out a press release to the local newspapers, websites and blogs. Several of the bars mentioned in this book have done an excellent job of making menu releases into an anticipated event that garners the attention of numerous press outlets.

One of your suppliers mentions that a national spirits brand ambassador will be passing through? See if you can turn it into a tasting event or pairing dinner, which you could promote to guests and on social media.

A Few Thoughts On Marketing

Marketing may seem slightly easier than public relations to attempt to do with no formal training—after all anyone can purchase some ads and post on social media, right? But in practice it's actually even more difficult than PR to do effectively, if you don't know what you're doing.

There are many great books on marketing out there, and you can find several recommendations on the book website. I highly encourage doing as much reading on marketing as you can if you're planning on handling it for your bar. That said, here are a few basics that are key to effective food & beverage marketing.

Utilize All Major Platforms

There are enough technologies available now to assist in social media management that there's no excuse for not having a presence across at least Instagram, Twitter and Facebook.

With minimal setup time you can utilize tools to cross-post to different social media platforms. It's important, in many cases, to personalize the post for each medium. But if you're just starting out it's key to at least establish a presence—which is easier than ever.

Cohesive Voice
It's important that you develop a voice for your brand. I've seen bars that might let several different managers make posts on social media, which nearly always results in a mishmash of different voices, styles and types of humor. All of which only serves to confuse your audience in the long run.

In my businesses we create a four-point Brand Persona list (one example: welcoming, classy, quirky, savvy) for each brand that our social media manager uses as a reference for all posts, newsletters, etc, to make sure they align correctly with the brand.

Position Your Brand Correctly
One of the core parts of a good marketing plan is having clarity about how your brand needs to be positioned in the marketplace in order to reach your target customers.

Maybe the goal is to establish the bar as a quirky place that has top-level drinks, or maybe it's that customers will have a unique experience, of which drinks are only a part.

Every use case will require a different approach, but it should always be designed around what the brand needs.

Waste, & Other Concerns

We touched on this earlier, but it's hard to overstate the importance of watching carefully what gets thrown out.

Numerous owners mentioned this, and it's an example of a series of little things that can add up to significant amounts of money made or lost.

Here are a few examples of areas wherein waste should be monitored.

Beer

A 1/2 barrel keg of beer should typically yield around 120 pints, with some waste factored in (about 37 pints is the typical yield from a 1/6 barrel keg). There are many factors that can make taps pour badly (improper gas regulator settings and improper beer temperature are two of the big ones), and if you're regularly getting less than this amount of yield from your kegs it likely bears investigating.

Does your canned or bottled beer rotate quickly enough that you never have to throw any away due to spoilage?

Wine

Does your bar staff regularly throw out x bottles of by-the-glass wine because the bottle has been open too long? Does it mean you have too many wines available by the glass or is it an acceptable amount of waste?

Citrus

Fresh citrus juice doesn't have a very long shelf life, so it's important to closely watch your pars (the standard amount that is prepared each day for service) and make sure that you aren't over-prepping.

Food Waste

Most commercial restaurant kitchens throw something out

Bar Profile

Top of the Monk

92 Patton Ave., Asheville, NC 28801
www.topofthemonk.com

Now run by Kala Brooks, after being opened by the author, this classics-focused bar in Asheville is a great example of a small operation that runs extremely efficiently. With a total staff of six and a capacity of only 30, the bar makes every ingredient other than their spirits from scratch, and puts out tens of thousands of drinks each year for patrons who enjoy views of the Blue Ridge Mountains from the rooftop patio.

on a regular basis. You must make sure that yours is in an acceptable range, and continually monitor it.

Bartender Spillage

If your bartenders are using jiggers, as nearly all cocktail bars do now, that greatly reduces the chances for spillage, but they are never eliminated. Making sure that your per-bottle yields are correct is an important metric to track at all times.

There are numerous other areas (soap, bar towels, hand towels, etc etc) where waste has the capability to make an appreciable difference on the bottom line. The more conscious you are of where things may be wasted the greater chance your bottom line will be pleasing.

A Few Words on Security, Oversight & Honesty

The thing that will have the biggest effect on how your employees treat the monies of your business are the procedures that you establish and utilize for the oversight of cash handling. While I've seen successful operations that had lax cash handling policies, it's probably not going to work out well for anyone in the long run.

Thinking about cash handling policies brings to mind the old farmer's trope "good fences make for good neighbors." It's not that anyone in your employ would be dishonest per se, but the more you can remove the possibility of dishonesty then there's less chance it will occur. Here are a few things to consider.

Safe

This is fairly basic, but I've been surprised several times by fairly successful bars, with large amounts of cash coming in, that do not have a safe.

Security Cameras

There are several very reliable models of camera available now, which can be monitored via phone app from manufacturers such as Nest and Simplisafe.

Comp Policy

Some places (mine included) empower bartenders to give away a comp drink at the bartender's discretion, if they think it will alleviate a disgruntled customer or make a new fan. Others only allow comps on the approval of a manager.

One of the most common ways money can leave your bar is in the form of a drink that doesn't get paid for or rung into the POS.

Regardless of your approach to this, if you create clarity about your expectations among your staff and continue to reinforce it their behavior is more likely to match your desired outcome.

Let Staff Know How Much Things Cost

I've found that bartenders sometimes tend to be more

conscientious when they understand that certain glassware may cost $5 or more per piece.

Staff Communication

Whether you have a large, sprawling staff with multiple levels of managers or are an owner-managed place with only a few other employees, clear and efficient communication is always important.

The approaches to managing staff communication in the dozens of bars I spoke to ranged from a communal notebook or bulletin board, to a private Facebook group, to apps like Slack. No matter what approach you take, there are a few common elements that are important.

Be Able to Contact Everyone

Whether it's as simple as a private Facebook group, or with software such as Slack or Jolt, having an effective way to send messages to all staff (and know they were received) is a necessity on a regular basis.

Create a System For Feedback

Many owners mentioned the importance of providing a way for staff to make suggestions.

As the people who are directly interfacing with guests, the staff will often have insights into operating processes that can prove incredibly valuable. But don't think that just because they are aware of how something can be improved they will automatically make the suggestion.

It's important that they have both encouragement, and a clearly defined channel with which to propose ideas to management. Maybe that's a suggestion box in the office, maybe it's via email, maybe it's a few minutes at the staff meeting, but once established it's also important to remind employees about it on an ongoing basis.

Have Regular Meetings

Many owners also noted how crucial it was to their business to have regular staff meetings. Whether it's weekly or monthly (few people said they would be comfortable meeting less regularly than that), having your entire team together at once is a key step towards the efficient dissemination of information.

Some Thoughts Regarding Ongoing Training

The necessity and level of ongoing training will vary according to your concept. Many operators though, myself included, feel that ongoing training of the staff is an important element of creating an enduring bar.

Whether in specific spirits or drink categories, service, or any number of other things that might be important to your concept. Craig Nelson, of the bar Proof, in Charleston, SC, makes it a requirement that all staff members enter at least two cocktail competitions each year, in order to ensure that they're continually working on and refining their recipes.

Andrew Friedman of Liberty and Charlie Hodge of Sovereign Remedies both have an educational training for their staff each week. Other bars I talked to have staff focus on a particular spirit or area of drinks for a period of time, before moving on to another.

There were still other bars that did little formal ongoing training, and instead focused on improving the systems and processes of their service. Regardless of where on this spectrum your bar program falls, it's good to have a clear idea of what approach your concept will require.

Inspections & How to Live Through Them

It is always good policy to have someone on your staff who is Serv-Safe certified, and in many areas it is now required. Depending on where you are there may also be state mandated training in order to serve alcohol.

It's important to contact your local health department, and your state liquor commission to learn about what's required. I would also recommend finding out what additional resources are available in your area.

For example, will your local alcohol law enforcement agents come do a training for staff? Great—book it! It will both help ensure your staff is informed about the laws in your area, as well as make you look good in the eyes of the law enforcement as a pro-active owner. This is never a bad thing.

A final thought on health and alcohol rules: It's not that much effort to learn all of the applicable health and alcohol serving laws in your area. The investment in learning and following all of the rules is minimal compared to the potential consequences for being found in violation of a law or code.

Figure out how your local officials want things done and then do it correctly—it's the only viable long-term approach.

On Systems & Longevity

Once your business is open and running, and the initial frenzy of buildout and opening has died down, it's time to focus on systems. The quality of the systems in place—across every area—within a business are one of the key performance indicators of long-term success in this industry.

At a glance the term 'systems' may seem so over-arching as to be nebulous, and the fact is that systems (in practice) can take on many forms. The important thing is that they have a form.

Your system for tracking maintenance needs might be as simple as a notebook that bar staff writes down anything that's broken, or it might be as sophisticated as a form in an employee's only section of your website that automatically alerts several managers on staff via text message. In either case, the important thing is that there is a defined way of doing things, and that employees are aware of how it works.

Many of the things we've discussed in this book fall into the category of ongoing systems that, when created, help ensure that the business runs efficiently and profitably. The proper system in place for pricing cocktails will ensure that your profit margins are maintained on an ongoing basis. A good system for inventory means you always know if spirits are being wasted or given away too much (or if desired gross margins and prices need to be adjusted to allow for more waste or comps). The list goes on and on.

And to be frank, there are certainly bar businesses out there who operate successfully without a wealth of great systems in place. But there is a hidden cost that comes with a lack of systems. That cost may include turnover (a lack of systems can often lead to employee frustration), lost time dealing with issues that could have been avoided with foresight or a more efficient system, or any number of other things that, over time, become significant.

On These Things We've Covered

At this point you should have, in addition to the work from the previous sections:

✔ Plans for ensuring the consistency and quality of your offering

✔ Systems for the management of your finances, waste, communication and any number of other things.

✔ A sustainable business, with vision and direction. My hat is off to you, for all of your hard work. Cheers!

A BRIEF FINAL WORD

In the course of writing this book I conducted dozens of interviews, with bar owners from all across the country, and almost every single one of them made a point of mentioning the same thing: business skills.

Many of the successful bar owners I spoke to had worked their way up in the industry, and hadn't received any formal business training prior to bar ownership. But there was near universal agreement that business education is the single most important thing necessary for an owner to be successful.

In every interview I asked what skill was most crucial to being a successful owner and most of the answers were similar, despite the various markets and sizes of the operations over which the interviewees presided. Over and over the responses were things such as "accounting," "business skills," "cash flow management," "management," and other similar standard areas of business.

And, since we're nearing the end of this book, that's perhaps the one point I want to make most clearly: know more than you need to about every aspect of *business* that relates to owning a bar, especially as it relates to the financials. This will have the single greatest effect on your success.

There are many great resources available, and the more of them you take advantage of, the better your chances of survival. More than one interviewee I spoke with talked about getting help from their local chapter of SCORE.

Others talked about taking courses on accounting or human resources, or finding business-focused books that addressed gaps in their knowledge. Don't know enough about accounting? Try to schedule an appointment with a CPA who has experience working with restaurants to learn what areas they think are most important.

Beyond the overarching fact of business knowledge, your success in this business is often made or broken based on an accumulation of small details. Are you getting the best deal possible on bar towels and cleaning supplies? Does your menu do a good enough job of cross-utilization of perishables to ensure that there is minimal waste? Is the host making sure people feel welcome and their experience starts well? Are the bartenders making the drinks as quickly and efficiently as possible? Does the mood of the room feel welcoming?

Most failures in the bar and restaurant industry are not because of one single, catastrophic misstep. Just as most airline crashes are not due to one fatal mistake by the pilots, but a series of small errors, so it is with bars.

And ultimately it's about looking at each detail, questioning it, asking if there's a way it can be improved. Hopefully then you come to a point where you realize that the improvements you're trying to make are no longer major things, but little fine-tunings.

And now we come to the end of our journey. I've done my best to combine hundreds of interviews, conversations and notes into these pages, and I can only hope that they're helpful to you in your endeavour.

The methods and practices I've described in these pages certainly don't guarantee success in the bar industry, but

What is the biggest reason bars fail?

"Mismanagement of the business side."

"Because owners opened the bar they wanted to open, not what the neighborhood needed."

"Labor costs and rent costs."

"Poor accounting and bookkeeping."

"Not watching their money."
—Josh Mazza, Seamstress, NYC

every single example represents things that have worked for bar operators who have achieved success in this industry.

The bar business is one of continual growth, challenges, and interesting problems—and as I said at the beginning, I wouldn't trade it for anything. I suspect that if you've made it this far and still want to open a bar, the same might be true for you as well.

There's nothing quite like the feeling of seeing lots of people enjoy something you've worked so hard to create. I wish you nothing but the best for your bar, and if I can help in any way, feel free to find me. It will be my pleasure to someday enjoy a cocktail in your place.

I wish you way more than luck.

— END —

ACKNOWLEGEMENTS

There are many many people whose efforts, expertise and guidance helped make this book a reality. A mere couple of pages is not sufficient to thank them, but I shall try. Firstly, thanks to Bill, Christy, Gail, Drew and all of the folks at White Mule Press and ADI for their support of and belief in this project.

I had many interesting conversations with operators and other folks from this industry during the writing of this book, and I greatly appreciate the insights, experience and wisdom from Jeff Bell, Neal Bodenheimer, Kala Brooks, Martin Cate, Erick Castro, Dale Degroff, Eben Freeman, Andrew Friedman, Kaleena Goldsworthy, Kenta Goto, Josh Harris, Charlie Hodge, Josh Mazza, Mickey Moran, Craig Nelson, Max Poppel, Brooks Reitz, Dan Rose, and Danny Shapiro.

My mother's support and babysitting were crucial, as were the feedback and encouragement of many many friends, especially Guthrie Bunn, Tracey Johnston-Crum, Drew Jones, Erik Moellering, and Paul Nunan.

Rich Cundiff's thoughtful and considered feedback on several versions of this manuscript was indispensable. Thanks to Dennis Kiingati, for asking me to recommend a book on cocktail bar operation—here it is, friend.

Jay Sanders is a business partner par excellence, and I can't imagine doing anything (especially this book) without being able to kick ideas around with him on a daily basis.

BIBLIOGRAPHY

Arnold, Dave. *Liquid Intelligence: The Art & Science of the Perfect Cocktail*. New York: W.W. Norton & Co., 2014

AvroKo. *Best Ugly: Restaurant Concepts & Architecture by AvroKo*. New York: HarperCollins, 2008.

Cate, Martin, and Rebecca Cate. *Smuggler's Cove: Exotic Cocktails, Rum, and the Cult of Tiki*. Berkeley: Ten Speed Press, 2016.

Chernev, Alexander. *The Marketing Plan Handbook*. Chicago: Cerebellum Press, 2011.

Collins, Jim. *Good to Great: Why Some Companies Make the Leap and Others Don't*. New York: HarperCollins, 2001.

Fields, Roger. *Restaurant Success By The Numbers*. Berkeley: Ten Speed Press, 2014.

Gerber, Michael. *The E-Myth Revisited: Why Most Small Businesses Don't Work and What to Do About It*. New York: HarperCollins, 1995.

Grove, Andrew S. *High Output Management*. New York: Vintage, 1995.

Horowitz, Ben. *The Hard Thing About Hard Things: Building a Business When There Are No Easy Answers*. New York: HarperCollins, 2014.

Johnson, Harry. *Bartenders' Manual and a Guide for Hotels & Restaurants*. New York: self-published, 1900.

Kaplan, David, Nick Fauchald, and Alex Day. *Death & Co: Modern Classic Cocktails*. Berkeley: Ten Speed Press, 2014.

Katz, Jeff B. *Restaurant Planning, Design & Construction: A Survival Manual For Owners, Operators, and Developers*. Hoboken: Wiley, 1997.

Lencioni, Patrick. *The Four Obsessions of an Extraordinary Executive.* San Francisco: Jossey-Bass, 2000.

Meehan, Jim, and Chris Gall. *The PDT Cocktail Book: The Complete Bartender's Guide from the Celebrated Speakeasy.* New York: Sterling Epicure, 2011.

Meyer, Danny. *Setting The Table: The Transforming Power of Hospitality in Business.* New York: HarperCollins, 2006.

Morgenthaler, Jeffrey, and Martha Holmberg. *The Bar Book: Elements of Cocktail Technique.* San Francisco: Chronicle Books, 2014.

Regan, Gary. *The Joy of Mixology: The Consummate Guide to the Bartender's Craft.* New York: Clarkson Potter, 2003.

Ries, Al and Jack Trout. *The 22 Immutable Laws of Marketing: Violate Them at Your Own Risk!* New York: HarperCollins, 1994.

Schmidgall, Raymond, David K. Hayes and Jack D. Ninemeier. *Restaurant Financial Basics.* Hoboken: Wiley, 2002.

Weinzweig, Ari. *Zingerman's Guide to Giving Great Service.* New York: Hyperion: 2004.

Lightning Source UK Ltd.
Milton Keynes UK
UKHW051041240921
390902UK00009B/184/J